BAPTISM

SOME CHURCHES HAVE A BAPTISTRY

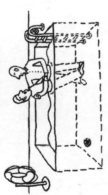

- 😊 BODY COMPLETELY IMMERSED - MORE OF A SPECTACLE

- 😊 BAPTISTRY CAN BE HIDDEN AWAY WHEN NOT IN USE

- 😊 BIBLE STORIES INVOLVING LARGE BODIES OF WATER CAN BE RE-ENACTED

- 😕 WATER METER-RELATED ISSUES AND PROBLEMS TO DO WITH ALL THE HOT WATER BEING USED UP

- 😕 DANGER OF SEEING THE VICAR'S KNEES

OTHER CHURCHES USE A FONT

- 😊 WATER POURED OR SPRINKLED - LESS DRIPPING

- 😊 NOT MUCH WATER NEEDED

- 😊 BIBLE STORIES INVOLVING SMALL BODIES OF WATER CAN BE RE-ENACTED

- 😕 BIBLICAL BASIS A BIT QUESTIONABLE

- 😕 FONT CAN GET IN THE WAY OF THE AREA WE USE TO HAVE COFFEE

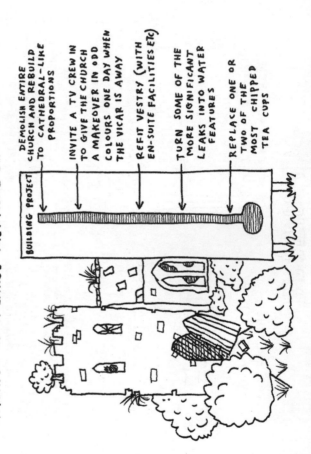

THE BUILDING PROJECT

SOMETIMES SOME MONEY NEEDS TO BE RAISED FOR A
CHURCH BUILDING PROJECT. THE AMOUNT THAT CAN BE
ACHIEVED WITH THE MONEY RAISED SO FAR IS TRADITIONALLY
DISPLAYED ON A LARGE THERMOMETER:

DEMOLISH ENTIRE
CHURCH AND REBUILD
TO CATHEDRAL-LIKE
PROPORTIONS

INVITE A TV CREW IN
TO GIVE THE CHURCH
A MAKEOVER IN ODD
COLOURS ONE DAY WHEN
THE VICAR IS AWAY

REFIT VESTRY (WITH
EN-SUITE FACILITIES ETC)

TURN SOME OF THE
MORE SIGNIFICANT
LEAKS INTO WATER
FEATURES

REPLACE ONE OR
TWO OF THE
MOST CHIPPED
TEA CUPS

BUILDING PROJECT

CATHEDRALS

CHURCH

CATHEDRAL

A CATHEDRAL IS LIKE A CHURCH, BUT ON A GRANDER SCALE

PEOPLE COME FROM ALL OVER THE WORLD TO RECORD THE ARCHITECTURAL FEATURES WITH THEIR CAMCORDERS

NO ENTRANCE WITHOUT A VOLUNTARY DONATION

IT COSTS A FORTUNE TO MAINTAIN A CATHERAL, SO YOU HAVE TO PAY TO GO IN

AUTHENTIC CATHEDRAL ODOUR

BUT IN RETURN THE STAFF DO ALL THEY CAN TO MAKE YOUR VISIT ENJOYABLE

THE CHAIN OF COMMAND

WITHIN A CHURCH

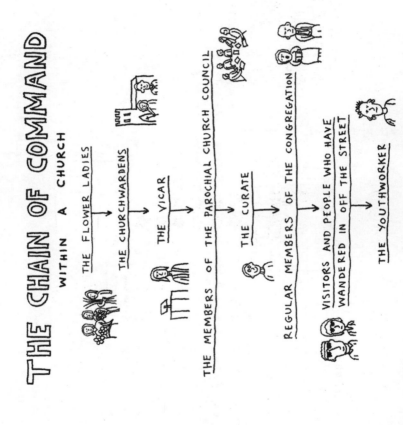

THE FLOWER LADIES

THE CHURCHWARDENS

THE VICAR

THE MEMBERS OF THE PAROCHIAL CHURCH COUNCIL

THE CURATE

REGULAR MEMBERS OF THE CONGREGATION

VISITORS AND PEOPLE WHO HAVE WANDERED IN OFF THE STREET

THE YOUTHWORKER

CHOIRS / MUSIC GROUPS
WHICH ARE THE BEST?

I HAVE UNDERTAKEN SOME IN-DEPTH ANALYSIS BASED ON THE FOLLOWING CATEGORIES:

CHOIRS  **MUSIC GROUPS**

	CHOIRS	MUSIC GROUPS
INSTRUMENTAL VARIETY	☆	☆☆☆
QUALITY OF ATTIRE	☆☆☆☆	☆☆
ABILITY TO PROCESS IN	☆☆☆☆	☆
HYMNS	☆☆☆☆	☆☆
CHORUSES	☆☆☆	☆☆☆☆
ABILITY TO DO ACTIONS TO CHILDRENS SONGS (AND AVOID THE DANGERS INHERENT THEREIN)	☆	☆☆
TOTALS →	**19**	**19**

WHICH, REMARKABLY, COME TO THE SAME NUMBER, THEREBY AVOIDING SCHISMS IN CHURCHES THROUGHOUT THE COUNTRY

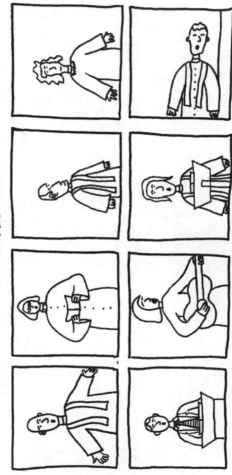

CHRISTMAS SERVICES

THERE ARE SO MANY SERVICES IN CHURCH OVER THE CHRISTMAS PERIOD THAT IT IS QUITE DIFFICULT TO FIND ENOUGH CLERGY TO CONDUCT THEM ALL.

SOME DIOCESES ARE RUMOURED TO BE EXPERIMENTING WITH CARDBOARD REPLICAS. AS YOU CAN SEE ONLY THE KEENEST EYE CAN TELL WHICH IS WHICH

CHRISTIAN UNITY

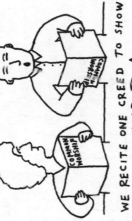

WE RECITE ONE CREED TO SHOW THAT WE HOLD TO A COMMON BELIEF

WE SHARE ONE BREAD TO DEMONSTRATE THAT WE ARE ONE BODY

WE LOVE EACH OTHER AS WE LOVE OUR OWN CHILDREN

WE SHARE THE PEACE TO SHOW THAT THERE ARE NO DISAGREEMENTS IN OUR MIDST

CHURCH BUILDINGS

SOME CHURCHES
HAVE STEEPLES

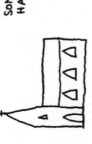

SOME CHURCHES
HAVE TOWERS

SOME CHURCHES
MEET IN HOUSES

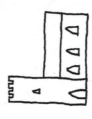

I ONCE HEARD
OF A CHURCH
WHICH MET
IN A CINEMA
BUT I THINK
THAT WAS
MADE UP

SOME CHURCHES MEET
IN SMALL BUILDINGS
THAT LOOK LIKE A GARDEN
SHED. BE WARNED THOUGH,
IF YOU SEE SPADES AND AN
OLD WHEELBARROW WHEN
YOU GO IN IT PROBABLY
IS A GARDEN SHED

OF COURSE THE
BUILDING IS NOT REALLY
THE IMPORTANT THING.
EXCEPT WHEN
IT IS RAINING

CHURCH GROWTH
POSSIBLE SCENARIOS

EACH DOT REPRESENTS ABOUT 34 CHURCHES

CURRENT SITUATION

CHURCH GROWTH (CAUSED BY FREE VOUCHERS, NOTHING GOOD ON TV ETC)

CHURCH DECLINE (CAUSED BY WELCOMERS NOT LOOKING LIKE THEY MEAN IT, HEATING NOT WORKING ETC)

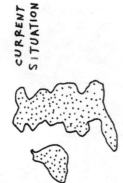

ALL WORSHIPPERS MOVING TO AREA IMMEDIATELY SURROUNDING MILTON KEYNES

[ALL NUMBERS ARE APPROXIMATE. GEOGRAPHY IS A BIT SKETCHY.]

THE CHURCH HALL

DEFINITION: A PEW-FREE ECCLESIASTICAL BUILDING
ENTIRELY SURROUNDED BY RESIDENTS WHO DON'T
LIKE NOISE. TYPICAL FEATURES INCLUDE:

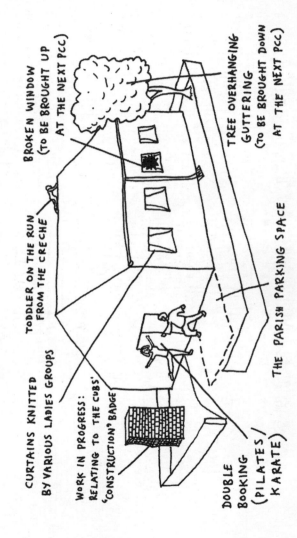

BROKEN WINDOW
(TO BE BROUGHT UP
AT THE NEXT PCC)

TREE OVERHANGING
GUTTERING
(TO BE BROUGHT DOWN
AT THE NEXT PCC)

TODDLER ON THE RUN
FROM THE CRECHE

CURTAINS KNITTED
BY VARIOUS LADIES GROUPS

WORK IN PROGRESS:
RELATING TO THE CUBS'
'CONSTRUCTION' BADGE

THE PARISH PARKING SPACE

DOUBLE
BOOKING
(PILATES/
KARATE)

THE CHURCH KITCHEN

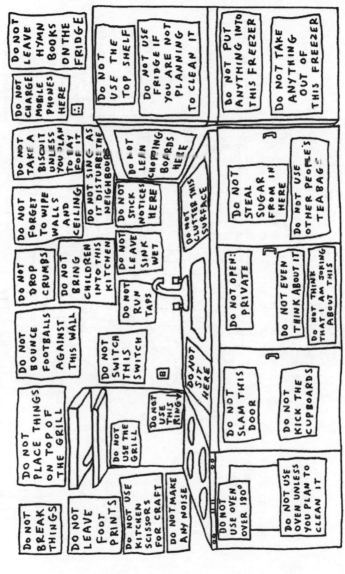

THE CHURCH OFFICE

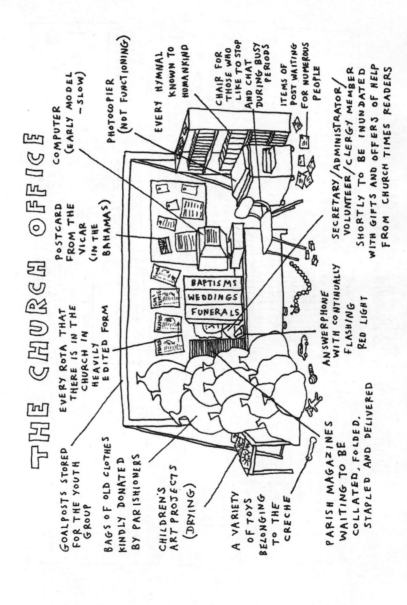

COMPUTER (EARLY MODEL – SLOW)

POSTCARD FROM THE VICAR (IN THE BAHAMAS)

PHOTOCOPIER (NOT FUNCTIONING)

EVERY HYMNAL KNOWN TO HUMANKIND

CHAIR FOR THOSE WHO LIKE TO STOP AND CHAT DURING BUSY PERIODS

ITEMS OF POST WAITING FOR NUMEROUS PEOPLE

SECRETARY/ADMINISTRATOR/ VOLUNTEER/CLERGY MEMBER SHORTLY TO BE INUNDATED WITH GIFTS AND OFFERS OF HELP FROM CHURCH TIMES READERS

EVERY ROTA THAT THERE IS IN THE CHURCH IN HEAVILY EDITED FORM

GOALPOSTS STORED FOR THE YOUTH GROUP

BAGS OF OLD CLOTHES KINDLY DONATED BY PARISHIONERS

CHILDREN'S ART PROJECTS (DRYING)

A VARIETY OF TOYS BELONGING TO THE CRECHE

PARISH MAGAZINES WAITING TO BE COLLATED, FOLDED, STAPLED AND DELIVERED

ANSWERPHONE WITH CONTINUALLY FLASHING RED LIGHT

BAPTISMS
WEDDINGS
FUNERALS

THE CHURCH ORGAN

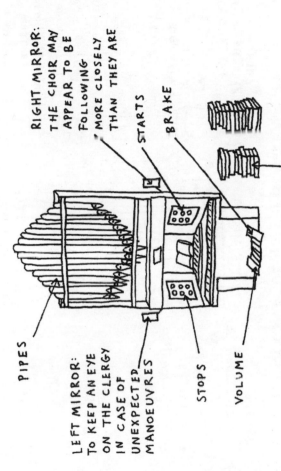

RIGHT MIRROR:
THE CHOIR MAY
APPEAR TO BE
FOLLOWING
MORE CLOSELY
THAN THEY ARE

STARTS

BRAKE

PIPES

LEFT MIRROR:
TO KEEP AN EYE
ON THE CLERGY
IN CASE OF
UNEXPECTED
MANOEUVRES

STOPS

VOLUME

NUMEROUS HYMNALS FOR EMERGENCY USE
IN THE EVENT OF UNSCHEDULED DIVERSIONS

CHURCH POLITICS

EXPLAINED USING CHESS PIECES

BISHOP:
MOVES DIAGONALLY.
COMES INTO PLAY
EVERY NOW AND
THEN FOR
CONFIRMATIONS
ETC

VICAR:
FOR EVERY
STEP FORWARD
TAKES TWO
TO THE SIDE.
LOOKS A BIT
LIKE A HORSE

CHURCH
FIXTURES AND
FITTINGS:

MAY NOT BE
MOVED
WITHOUT
A FACULTY

ORDINARY
CHURCHGOER:
LOTS OF THEM,
MOVE SLOWLY
IN ONE
DIRECTION.
FAIRLY
DISPENSABLE

CHURCHWARDEN:
MOST
POWERFUL
PIECE.
CAN ATTACK
IN ANY
DIRECTION

THIS PIECE
IS THE ONE WE
ARE TRYING
TO PROTECT.
I FORGET WHAT
IT IS CALLED

CHURCHWARDENS

THESE ARE SOME OF THEIR MAIN DUTIES

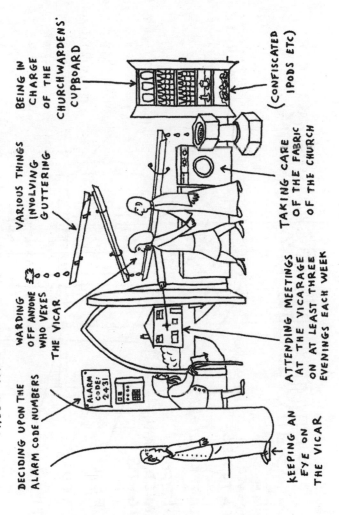

VARIOUS THINGS INVOLVING GUTTERING

BEING IN CHARGE OF THE CHURCHWARDENS' CUPBOARD

(CONFISCATED IPODS ETC)

TAKING CARE OF THE FABRIC OF THE CHURCH

WARDING OFF ANYONE WHO VEXES THE VICAR

DECIDING UPON THE ALARM CODE NUMBERS

ALARM CODE: 2431

ATTENDING MEETINGS AT THE VICARAGE ON AT LEAST THREE EVENINGS EACH WEEK

KEEPING AN EYE ON THE VICAR

CHURCH WINDOWS

SOME
COMMON
FEATURES:

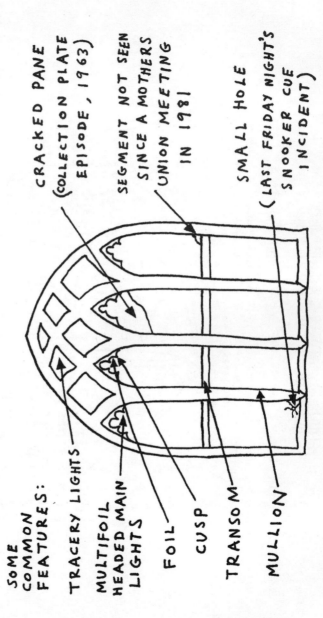

TRACERY LIGHTS

MULTIFOIL
HEADED MAIN
LIGHTS

FOIL

CUSP

TRANSOM

MULLION

CRACKED PANE
(COLLECTION PLATE
EPISODE, 1963)

SEGMENT NOT SEEN
SINCE A MOTHERS
UNION MEETING
IN 1981

SMALL HOLE
(LAST FRIDAY NIGHT'S
SNOOKER CUE
INCIDENT)

BAPTISM

SOME CHURCHES HAVE A BAPTISTRY

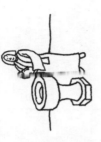

OTHER CHURCHES USE A FONT

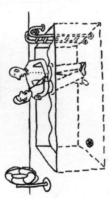

☺ BODY COMPLETELY IMMERSED – MORE OF A SPECTACLE

☺ BAPTISTRY CAN BE HIDDEN AWAY WHEN NOT IN USE

☺ BIBLE STORIES INVOLVING LARGE BODIES OF WATER CAN BE RE-ENACTED

☹ WATER METER-RELATED ISSUES AND PROBLEMS TO DO WITH ALL THE HOT WATER BEING USED UP

☹ DANGER OF SEEING THE VICAR'S KNEES

☺ WATER POURED OR SPRINKLED – LESS TRIPPING

☺ NOT MUCH WATER NEEDED

☺ BIBLE STORIES INVOLVING SMALL BODIES OF WATER CAN BE RE-ENACTED

☹ BIBLICAL OASIS A BIT QUESTIONABLE

☹ FONT CAN GET IN THE WAY OF THE AREA WE USE TO HAVE COFFEE

THE BUILDING PROJECT

SOMETIMES SOME MONEY NEEDS TO BE RAISED FOR A CHURCH BUILDING PROJECT. THE AMOUNT THAT CAN BE ACHIEVED WITH THE MONEY RAISED SO FAR IS TRADITIONALLY DISPLAYED ON A LARGE THERMOMETER:

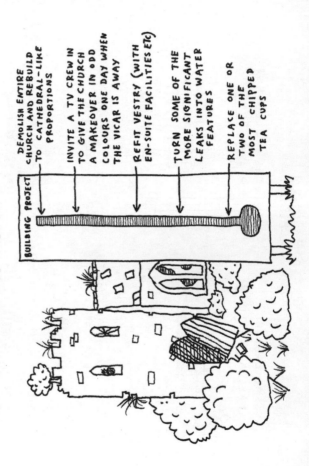

DEMOLISH ENTIRE CHURCH AND REBUILD TO CATHEDRAL-LIKE PROPORTIONS

INVITE A TV CREW IN TO GIVE THE CHURCH A MAKEOVER IN ODD COLOURS ONE DAY WHEN THE VICAR IS AWAY

REFIT VESTRY (WITH EN-SUITE FACILITIES ETC)

TURN SOME OF THE MORE SIGNIFICANT LEAKS INTO WATER FEATURES

REPLACE ONE OR TWO OF THE MOST CHIPPED TEA CUPS

BUILDING PROJECT

CATHEDRALS

CATHEDRAL

CHURCH

A CATHEDRAL IS LIKE A CHURCH,
BUT ON A GRANDER SCALE

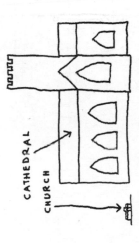

PEOPLE COME FROM ALL OVER
THE WORLD TO RECORD THE
ARCHITECTURAL FEATURES
WITH THEIR CAMCORDERS

NO ENTRANCE
WITHOUT A
VOLUNTARY
DONATION

IT COSTS A FORTUNE TO MAINTAIN
A CATHERAL, SO YOU HAVE TO
PAY TO GO IN

AUTHENTIC
CATHEDRAL
ODOUR

BUT IN RETURN THE STAFF DO
ALL THEY CAN TO MAKE
YOUR VISIT ENJOYABLE

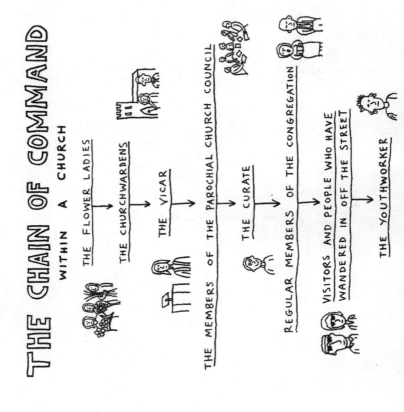

THE CHAIN OF COMMAND

WITHIN A CHURCH

THE FLOWER LADIES

THE CHURCHWARDENS

THE VICAR

THE MEMBERS OF THE PAROCHIAL CHURCH COUNCIL

THE CURATE

REGULAR MEMBERS OF THE CONGREGATION

VISITORS AND PEOPLE WHO HAVE WANDERED IN OFF THE STREET

THE YOUTHWORKER

CHOIRS / MUSIC GROUPS
WHICH ARE THE BEST?

I HAVE UNDERTAKEN
SOME IN-DEPTH
ANALYSIS BASED
ON THE FOLLOWING
CATEGORIES:

CHOIRS

MUSIC GROUPS

INSTRUMENTAL VARIETY

QUALITY OF ATTIRE

ABILITY TO PROCESS IN

HYMNS

CHORUSES

ABILITY TO DO ACTIONS
TO CHILDRENS SONGS
(AND AVOID THE DANGERS INHERENT THEREIN)

TOTALS

WHICH, REMARKABLY,
COME TO THE SAME
NUMBER, THEREBY AVOIDING
SCHISMS IN CHURCHES
THROUGHOUT THE COUNTRY

19   19

CHRISTMAS SERVICES

THERE ARE SO MANY SERVICES IN CHURCH OVER THE CHRISTMAS PERIOD THAT IT IS QUITE DIFFICULT TO FIND ENOUGH CLERGY TO CONDUCT THEM ALL.

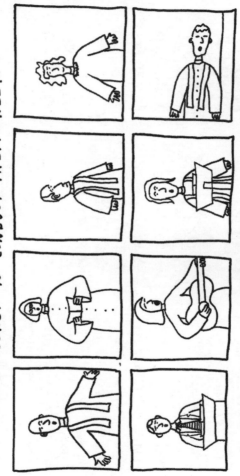

SOME DIOCESES ARE RUMOURED TO BE EXPERIMENTING WITH CARDBOARD REPLICAS. AS YOU CAN SEE ONLY THE KEENEST EYE CAN TELL WHICH IS WHICH

CHRISTIAN UNITY

WE RECITE ONE CREED TO SHOW THAT WE HOLD TO A COMMON BELIEF

WILL YOU JUST **LISTEN!!**

WE LOVE EACH OTHER AS WE LOVE OUR OWN CHILDREN

WE SHARE ONE BREAD TO DEMONSTRATE THAT WE ARE ONE BODY

WE SHARE THE PEACE TO SHOW THAT THERE ARE NO DISAGREEMENTS IN OUR MIDST

CHURCH BUILDINGS

SOME CHURCHES
HAVE STEEPLES

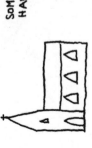

SOME CHURCHES
HAVE TOWERS

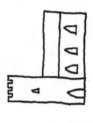

SOME CHURCHES
MEET IN HOUSES

SOME CHURCHES MEET
IN SMALL BUILDINGS
THAT LOOK LIKE A GARDEN
SHED. BE WARNED THOUGH,
IF YOU SEE SPADES AND AN
OLD WHEELBARROW WHEN
YOU GO IN IT PROBABLY
IS A GARDEN SHED

I ONCE HEARD
OF A CHURCH
WHICH MET
IN A CINEMA
BUT I THINK
THAT WAS
MADE UP

OF COURSE THE
BUILDING IS NOT REALLY
THE IMPORTANT THING.
EXCEPT WHEN
IT IS RAINING

CHURCH GROWTH

POSSIBLE SCENARIOS

EACH DOT REPRESENTS ABOUT 34 CHURCHES

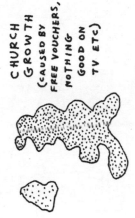

CURRENT SITUATION

CHURCH GROWTH (CAUSED BY FREE VOUCHERS, NOTHING GOOD ON TV ETC)

CHURCH DECLINE (CAUSED BY WELCOMERS NOT LOOKING LIKE THEY MEAN IT, HEATING NOT WORKING ETC)

ALL WORSHIPPERS MOVING TO AREA IMMEDIATELY SURROUNDING MILTON KEYNES

[ALL NUMBERS ARE APPROXIMATE. GEOGRAPHY IS A BIT SKETCHY.]

THE CHURCH HALL

DEFINITION: A PEW-FREE ECCLESIASTICAL BUILDING ENTIRELY SURROUNDED BY RESIDENTS WHO DON'T LIKE NOISE. TYPICAL FEATURES INCLUDE:

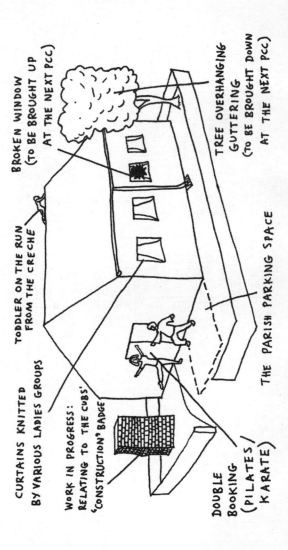

CURTAINS KNITTED BY VARIOUS LADIES GROUPS

TODDLER ON THE RUN FROM THE CRECHE

BROKEN WINDOW (TO BE BROUGHT UP AT THE NEXT PCC)

WORK IN PROGRESS: RELATING TO THE CUBS' 'CONSTRUCTION' BADGE

TREE OVERHANGING GUTTERING (TO BE BROUGHT DOWN AT THE NEXT PCC)

DOUBLE BOOKING (PILATES / KARATE)

THE PARISH PARKING SPACE

THE CHURCH KITCHEN

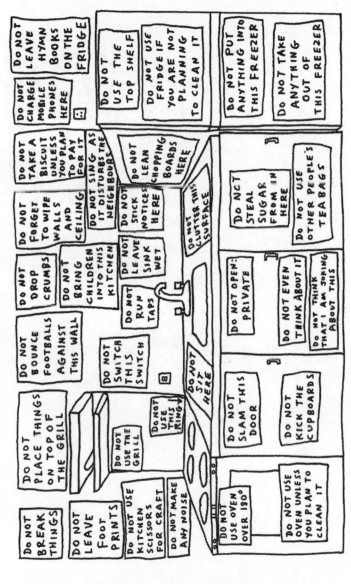

THE CHURCH OFFICE

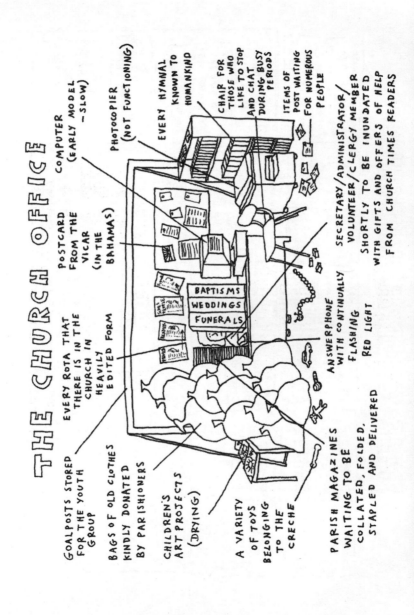

COMPUTER (EARLY MODEL – SLOW)

POSTCARD FROM THE VICAR (IN THE BAHAMAS)

PHOTOCOPIER (NOT FUNCTIONING)

EVERY HYMNAL KNOWN TO HUMANKIND

CHAIR FOR THOSE WHO LIKE TO STOP AND CHAT DURING BUSY PERIODS

ITEMS OF POST WAITING FOR NUMEROUS PEOPLE

SECRETARY/ADMINISTRATOR/ VOLUNTEER/CLERGY MEMBER SHORTLY TO BE INUNDATED WITH GIFTS AND OFFERS OF HELP FROM CHURCH TIMES READERS

GOALPOSTS STORED FOR THE YOUTH GROUP

EVERY ROTA THAT THERE IS IN THE CHURCH IN HEAVILY EDITED FORM

BAGS OF OLD CLOTHES KINDLY DONATED BY PARISHIONERS

CHILDREN'S ART PROJECTS (DRYING)

A VARIETY OF TOYS BELONGING TO THE CRECHE

PARISH MAGAZINES WAITING TO BE COLLATED, FOLDED, STAPLED AND DELIVERED

ANSWERPHONE WITH CONTINUALLY FLASHING RED LIGHT

BAPTISMS WEDDINGS FUNERALS

THE CHURCH ORGAN

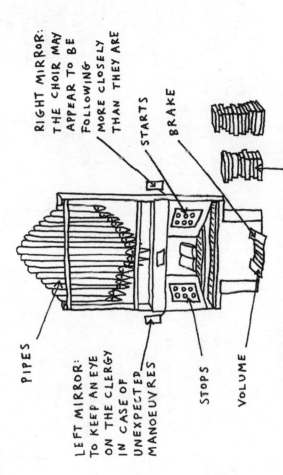

RIGHT MIRROR:
THE CHOIR MAY
APPEAR TO BE
FOLLOWING
MORE CLOSELY
THAN THEY ARE

STARTS

BRAKE

PIPES

LEFT MIRROR:
TO KEEP AN EYE
ON THE CLERGY
IN CASE OF
UNEXPECTED
MANOEUVRES

STOPS

VOLUME

NUMEROUS HYMNALS FOR EMERGENCY USE
IN THE EVENT OF UNSCHEDULED DIVERSIONS

CHURCH POLITICS
EXPLAINED USING CHESS PIECES

BISHOP:
MOVES DIAGONALLY.
COMES INTO PLAY
EVERY NOW AND
THEN FOR
CONFIRMATIONS
ETC

VICAR:
FOR EVERY
STEP FORWARD
TAKES TWO
TO THE SIDE.
LOOKS A BIT
LIKE A HORSE

CHURCH
FIXTURES AND
FITTINGS:

MAY NOT BE
MOVED
WITHOUT
A FACULTY

ORDINARY
CHURCHGOER:
LOTS OF THEM.
MOVE SLOWLY
IN ONE
DIRECTION.
FAIRLY
DISPENSABLE

CHURCHWARDEN:
MOST
POWERFUL
PIECE.
CAN ATTACK
IN ANY
DIRECTION

THIS PIECE
IS THE ONE WE
ARE TRYING
TO PROTECT.
I FORGET WHAT
IT IS CALLED

CHURCHWARDENS

THESE ARE SOME OF THEIR MAIN DUTIES

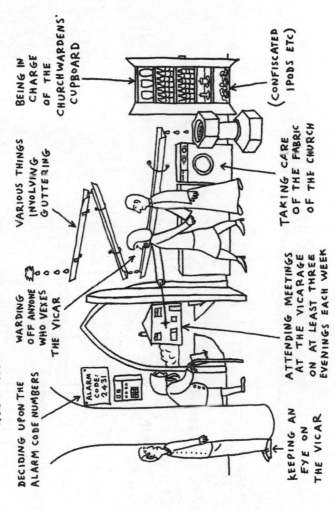

DECIDING UPON THE ALARM CODE NUMBERS

WARDING OFF ANYONE WHO VEXES THE VICAR

VARIOUS THINGS INVOLVING GUTTERING

BEING IN CHARGE OF THE CHURCHWARDENS' CUPBOARD

(CONFISCATED IPODS ETC)

TAKING CARE OF THE FABRIC OF THE CHURCH

ATTENDING MEETINGS AT THE VICARAGE ON AT LEAST THREE EVENINGS EACH WEEK

KEEPING AN EYE ON THE VICAR

ALARM CODE: 2431

CHURCH WINDOWS

SOME
COMMON
FEATURES:

TRACERY LIGHTS

MULTIFOIL
HEADED MAIN
LIGHTS

FOIL

CUSP

TRANSOM

MULLION

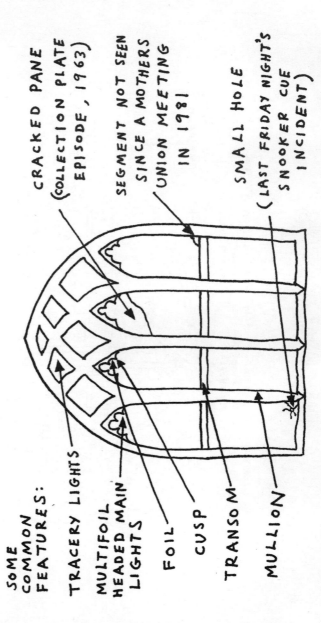

CRACKED PANE
(COLLECTION PLATE
EPISODE, 1963)

SEGMENT NOT SEEN
SINCE A MOTHERS
UNION MEETING
IN 1981

SMALL HOLE
(LAST FRIDAY NIGHT'S
SNOOKER CUE
INCIDENT)

COFFEE TIME

THERE IS QUITE OFTEN ONE OF THESE AFTER THE SERVICE

TO RUN ONE YOU WILL NEED:

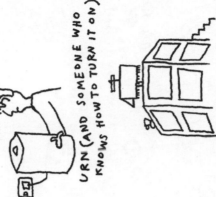

URN (AND SOMEONE WHO KNOWS HOW TO TURN IT ON)

ABILITY TO SPOT DISCARDED CUPS AND SAUCERS IN ODD AND SUNDRY PLACES

BISCUITS (PLAIN)

MILK (PLENTY)

TRAYS (FLORAL)

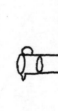

PALE GREEN CUPS AND SAUCERS

GIANT METAL TEAPOT FROM AGES PAST

COFFEE (WEAK)

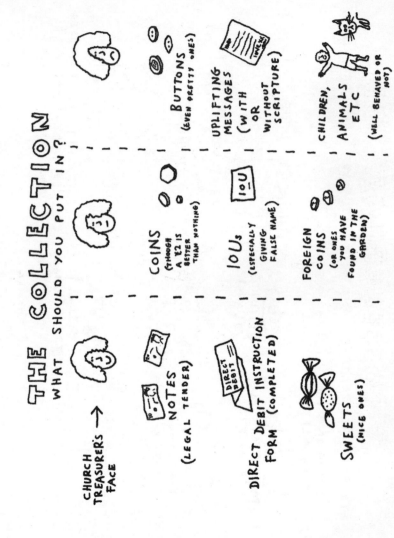

THE COLLECTION
WHAT SHOULD YOU PUT IN?

CHURCH TREASURER'S FACE →

NOTES
(LEGAL TENDER)

DIRECT DEBIT INSTRUCTION FORM (COMPLETED)

SWEETS
(NICE ONES)

COINS
(THOUGH A ₤2 IS BETTER THAN NOTHING)

IOUs
(ESPECIALLY GIVING FALSE NAME)

FOREIGN COINS
(OR ONES YOU HAVE FOUND IN THE GARDEN)

BUTTONS
(EVEN PRETTY ONES)

UPLIFTING MESSAGES
(WITH OR WITHOUT SCRIPTURE)

CHILDREN, ANIMALS ETC
(WELL BEHAVED OR NOT)

THE CONGREGATION

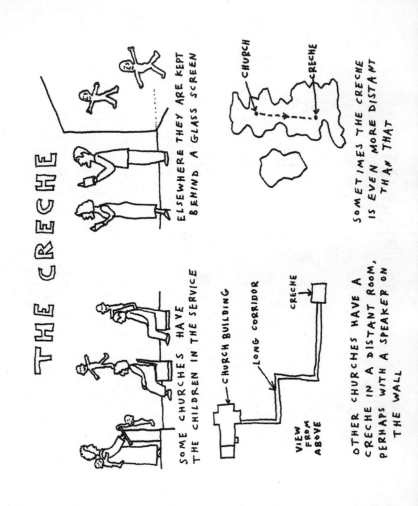

THE CRECHE

SOME CHURCHES HAVE
THE CHILDREN IN THE SERVICE

ELSEWHERE THEY ARE KEPT
BEHIND A GLASS SCREEN

CHURCH BUILDING
LONG CORRIDOR
CRECHE

VIEW
FROM
ABOVE

OTHER CHURCHES HAVE A
CRECHE IN A DISTANT ROOM,
PERHAPS WITH A SPEAKER ON
THE WALL

CHURCH
CRECHE

SOMETIMES THE CRECHE
IS EVEN MORE DISTANT
THAN THAT

FLAGS

A FLAG CAN BE FLOWN FROM THE CHURCH TOWER TO
CONVEY A NUMBER OF DIFFERENT MEANINGS:

THERE HAS BEEN SOME
SORT OF NATIONAL TRIUMPH
OR
WE LIKE TO FLY A FLAG

THERE HAS BEEN SOME
SORT OF NATIONAL TRAGEDY
OR
WE ARE HAVING PROBLEMS
WITH THE WINDING MECHANISM

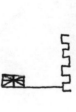

WE HAVE A NEW CHURCHWARDEN
WHO HAS NOT LEARNT
THE ROPES YET

WE SUPPORT
THE FOOTBALL

THE FLOWER FESTIVAL

UNDERSTANDING THE ARRANGEMENTS

DANIEL IN THE
LION'S DEN

CROSSING THE
RED SEA

PAUL'S THIRD
MISSIONARY JOURNEY

THE DAY OF
PENTECOST

THE HIERARCHY OF CLERGY

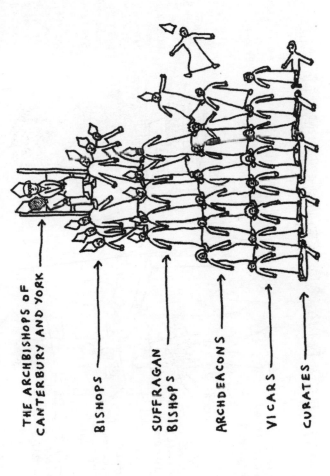

THE ARCHBISHOPS of
CANTERBURY AND YORK

BISHOPS

SUFFRAGAN
BISHOPS

ARCHDEACONS

VICARS

CURATES

HOW TO MAKE CHURCH BRILLIANT

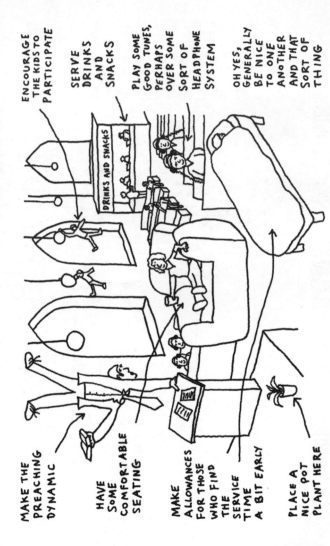

ENCOURAGE THE KIDS TO PARTICIPATE

SERVE DRINKS AND SNACKS

PLAY SOME GOOD TUNES, PERHAPS OVER SOME SORT OF HEADPHONE SYSTEM

OH YES, GENERALLY BE NICE TO ONE ANOTHER AND THAT SORT OF THING

MAKE THE PREACHING DYNAMIC

HAVE SOME COMFORTABLE SEATING

MAKE ALLOWANCES FOR THOSE WHO FIND THE SERVICE TIME A BIT EARLY

PLACE A NICE POT PLANT HERE

HOW TO TELL WHAT IS GOING ON

FIRST READING

SECOND READING

PRAYERS

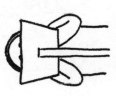

NOTICES

LENT

LENT IS A TIME FOR QUIET REFLECTION AND CONTEMPLATION

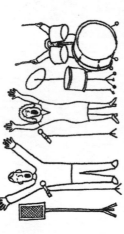

IT IS A SEASON OF ABSTINENCE AND FASTING

ALPHA SUPPER

SOME CHRISTIANS GIVE SOMETHING UP DURING LENT

OTHERS CHOOSE TO CARRY OUT ACTS OF PENANCE

THE LITURGICAL PAUSE

THIS IS ONE OF THE CENTRAL ELEMENTS OF A CHURCH SERVICE.
WE OBSERVE A LITURGICAL PAUSE AT THE FOLLOWING POINTS:

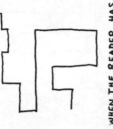

WHEN THE ORGANIST HASN'T COME IN

WHEN THE READER HAS A PARTICULARLY GRUELLING JOURNEY TO THE LECTERN

AT MOMENTS WHEN PONDERING IS EXPECTED

WHEN NO-ONE WILL ADMIT TO BEING THE PERSON DOWN TO LEAD THE INTERCESSIONS

WHEN NOBODY HAS A CLUE WHAT IS SUPPOSED TO HAPPEN NEXT

WHEN AN EASTER FIRE OR ADVENT CANDLE REFUSES TO LIGHT

LOST PROPERTY

THIS IS COLLECTED BY THE CHURCHWARDENS AND RETAINED FOR A
WEEK OR TWO BEFORE BEING SENT TO A GIANT CENTRAL WAREHOUSE
DEEP IN THE VAULTS OF CHURCH HOUSE

EVERY FEW MONTHS THE BISHOPS ARE ALLOWED TO HAVE A WANDER
ROUND AND CAN HELP THEMSELVES TO THE CHOICEST ITEMS

MICROPHONES

IT IS QUITE UNUSUAL TO FIND A CHURCH SOUND
SYSTEM THAT WORKS PROPERLY. THESE ARE THE ONLY
FULLY FUNCTIONING CHURCH MICROPHONES THAT
HAVE BEEN DOCUMENTED:

MICROPHONE
(NORTH OF ENGLAND)

NO FEEDBACK EVEN
DURING THE LOUD BITS

MICROPHONE (SCOTLAND)

NO HISSING
(FROM THE
MICROPHONE AT LEAST)

RADIO MICROPHONE
(LONDON)

SIGNAL UNAFFECTED
BY WEIGHTY
CASSOCK

RADIO MICROPHONE
(MIDLANDS)

SIGNAL CLEAR EVEN
WHEN SPEAKER HAS
WANDERED OFF

MICROPHONE
(NORTHERN IRELAND)

PRAYERS CAN BE
HEARD, EVEN IN THE
POPULAR BACK PEWS

PULPIT MICROPHONE
(WALES)

DOESN'T CUT OUT DURING
CRUCIAL SERMON SEGMENTS

NEW CLERGY

NEW CLERGY LIKE TO BE WELCOMED INTO THE PARISH WITH
A BOX CONTAINING THE FOLLOWING ITEMS:

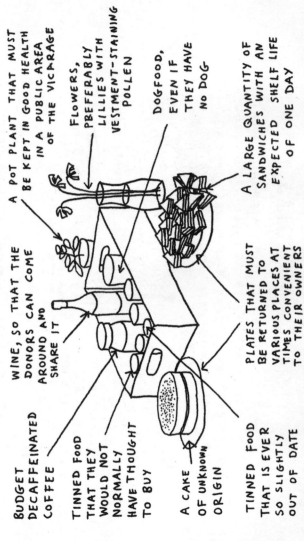

BUDGET
DECAFFEINATED
COFFEE

WINE, SO THAT THE
DONORS CAN COME
AROUND AND
SHARE IT

A POT PLANT THAT MUST
BE KEPT IN GOOD HEALTH
IN A PUBLIC AREA
OF THE VICARAGE

FLOWERS,
PREFERABLY
LILLIES WITH
VESTMENT-STAINING
POLLEN

DOGFOOD,
EVEN IF
THEY HAVE
NO DOG

A LARGE QUANTITY OF
SANDWICHES WITH AN
EXPECTED SHELF LIFE
OF ONE DAY

TINNED FOOD
THAT THEY
WOULD NOT
NORMALLY
HAVE THOUGHT
TO BUY

A CAKE
OF UNKNOWN
ORIGIN

PLATES THAT MUST
BE RETURNED TO
VARIOUS PLACES AT
TIMES CONVENIENT
TO THEIR OWNERS

TINNED FOOD
THAT IS EVER
SO SLIGHTLY
OUT OF DATE

NEW YEAR'S EVE

UNLIKE ADVENT AND CHRISTMAS NEW YEAR IS NOT ONE OF THE FESTIVALS OF THE CHRISTIAN YEAR

THIS MEANS THAT WHEN NEW YEAR'S DAY FALLS ON A SUNDAY THE PEWS WILL BE FULL OF BRIGHT-EYED WORSHIPPERS, KEEN TO FACE THE CHALLENGES THAT THE NEW YEAR BRINGS WITH VIGOUR AND ENTHUSIASM

UNDERSTANDING THE NUMBERS FOUND AT THE FRONT OF CHURCH

OFTEN YOU WILL SEE SOME NUMBERS ON BOARDS AT THE FRONT.
THESE MEAN DIFFERENT THINGS IN DIFFERENT CHURCHES. SOME POSSIBILITIES:

HYMNS

PSALMS

PEWLOTTO™ NUMBERS
CHECK WITH NUMBERS
ON SERVICE SHEET

NUMBERS OF PEOPLE
REQUIRED TO SERVE AS
PCC MEMBERS
DEANERY SYNOD REPS
SUNDAY SCHOOL TEACHERS
CHURCHWARDENS

BABY CRYING
IF YOUR CHILD MATCHES ONE
OF THESE NUMBERS COLLECT
THEM FROM THE SUNDAY SCHOOL
AS THINGS ARE NOT GOING WELL

THE NEXT
BUSES OUT
OF HERE

ORGANISTS

THERE ARE SEVERAL VARIETIES

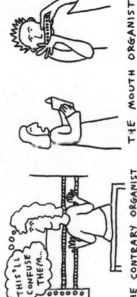

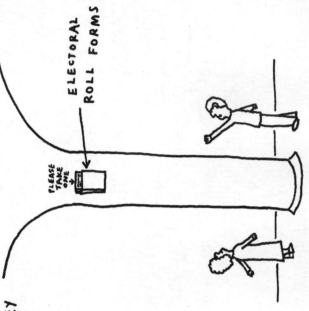

THE PARISH SHARE

THIS IS THE MONEY
EACH PARISH PAYS
TO THE DIOCESE
IN RETURN FOR
CLERGY ETC

CHURCHES WITH
FEWER PEOPLE ON
THE ELECTORAL
ROLL SOMETIMES
HAVE TO PAY
LESS PARISH
SHARE

ELECTORAL
ROLL FORMS

PLEASE
TAKE
ONE

THE P.C.C.

THE PAROCHIAL CHURCH COUNCIL MEETS EVERY NOW AND THEN TO DISCUSS THINGS TO DO WITH THE CHURCH. THESE ARE THE PEOPLE WHO ARE PART OF IT

DEANERY SYNOD REP.
USUALLY VOTED IN IN THEIR ABSENCE

YOUNG IDEALIST. PLANS TO CHANGE THE PCC, THE CHURCH AND ULTIMATELY THE WORLD. WILL LAST 5-6 MONTHS

TREASURER.
IT IS THEIR JOB TO SAY 'NO'.

DISSENTER.
SPOTS THE FAULTS IN ALL PROPOSALS AND ASKS DIFFICULT QUESTIONS AT THE ANNUAL GENERAL MEETING

VICAR. OFTEN THE CHAIR. GETS SAT ON BY THE CHURCHWARDENS

CLOCK WATCHER. JOB: TO ENSURE MEETING FINISHES AN HOUR BEFORE LAST ORDERS. USUALLY FAILS

CHURCHWARDENS
KEEPERS OF LAW, ORDER AND THE KEYS TO LOTS OF THINGS

SECRETARY
TAKES MINUTES. IT WOULD TAKE ME HOURS

INSPIRER OF TANGENTS AND POINTLESS DISCUSSIONS. ADDS 37 MINUTES TO AVERAGE MEETING

PEWS

THE DIFFERENT CLASSES

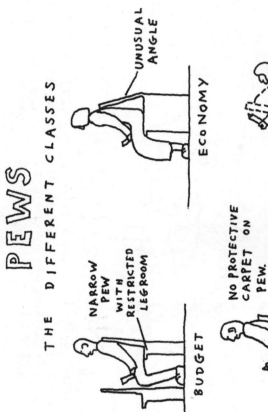

NARROW PEW WITH RESTRICTED LEGROOM

BUDGET

UNUSUAL ANGLE

ECONOMY

NO PROTECTIVE CARPET ON PEW. NUMBNESS STARTS HERE AND SPREADS

SAVER

RECLINING ACTION

FIRST CLASS

PEWS

HISTORICAL AND SUNDRY INFORMATION

IN THE OLD DAYS
PEWS WERE NUMBERED
AND PEOPLE COULD RENT
THEIR FAVOURITE.
THE ONES AT THE BACK
CHANGED HANDS FOR
A LOT OF MONEY

SOMETIMES
THEY HAD
DOORS TO
KEEP OUT
ANIMALS
AND STOP
PEOPLE WANDERING
AROUND TOO MUCH
DURING THE PEACE

OF COURSE
THESE DAYS
THINGS HAVE
CHANGED.
YOU WILL KNOW
IF YOU HAVE
TAKEN A PEW
BELONGING TO
SOMEONE ELSE BY
THE SPECIAL
CUSHION AND THE FUNNY
LOOKS PEOPLE ARE GIVING YOU

THE LEDGE IS TRADITIONALLY
JUST TOO NARROW TO PUT
ONES PRAYERBOOK DOWN.
THIS IS TO DISCOURAGE LOSING
ONES PLACE, TAKING PART IN
ACTION SONGS ETC

52

THE PULPIT

THESE ARE THE TYPICAL CONTROLS

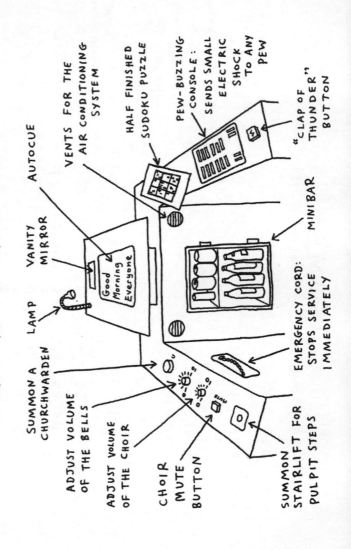

SUMMON A CHURCHWARDEN

ADJUST VOLUME OF THE BELLS

ADJUST VOLUME OF THE CHOIR

CHOIR MUTE BUTTON

SUMMON STAIRLIFT FOR PULPIT STEPS

LAMP

VANITY MIRROR

AUTOCUE

Good Morning Everyone

VENTS FOR THE AIR CONDITIONING SYSTEM

HALF FINISHED SUDOKU PUZZLE

PEW-BUZZING CONSOLE: SENDS SMALL ELECTRIC SHOCK TO ANY PEW

"CLAP OF THUNDER" BUTTON

EMERGENCY CORD: STOPS SERVICE IMMEDIATELY

MINIBAR

HOW TO RECOGNISE PEOPLE
BY THE KIND OF STICK THEY ARE CARRYING

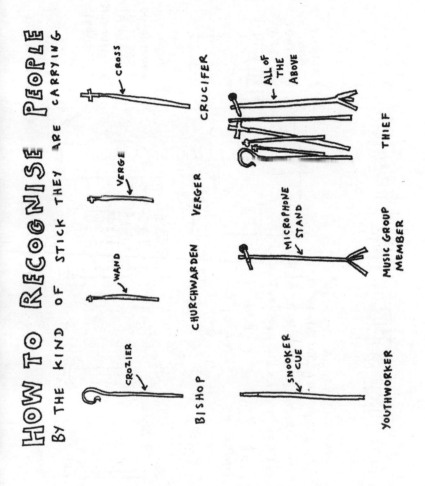

CROZIER — BISHOP

WAND — CHURCHWARDEN

VERGE — VERGER

CROSS — CRUCIFER

SNOOKER CUE — YOUTHWORKER

MICROPHONE STAND — MUSIC GROUP MEMBER

ALL OF THE ABOVE — THIEF

RESTRICTED AREAS

VISITORS TO A CHURCH
ARE GENERALLY ALLOWED
TO WANDER AROUND AS
THEY PLEASE. HOWEVER,
ONE OR TWO AREAS
MAY BE ROPED-OFF

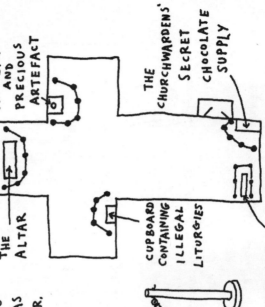

ANCIENT
AND
PRECIOUS
ARTEFACT

THE CHURCHWARDENS' SECRET CHOCOLATE SUPPLY

THE ALTAR

CUPBOARD CONTAINING ILLEGAL LITURGIES

THE VERGER'S WIFE'S FAVOURITE PEW

ROTAS

THE ROTA IS ONE OF THE CENTRAL INSTITUTIONS
OF THE CHURCH. WITHOUT THEM VERY LITTLE WOULD HAPPEN

WE STILL NEED PEOPLE FOR
THESE ROTAS. PLEASE SIGN UP
AT YOUR EARLIEST OPPORTUNITY

I AM SORRY BUT THESE
ROTAS ARE COMPLETELY FILLED.
TRY AGAIN NEXT YEAR PERHAPS

FLOWER ROTA
4
11
18
25

COFFEE ROTA
4
11
18
25

CLEANING ROTA
4
11
18
25

SIDESMANS ROTA
4
11
18
25

ADMIRING THE FLOWERS ROTA
4
11
18
25

DRINKING THE COFFEE ROTA
4
11
18
25

LOOKING OUT FOR WHERE THE CLEANERS MISSED A BIT ROTA
4
11
18
25

LOOKING ON FROM THE SIDELINES ROTA
4
11
18
25

RURAL MINISTRY

THIS IS THE ROUTE TAKEN BY A
RURAL MINISTER ON A TYPICAL
SUNDAY MORNING (AS SEEN
FROM A GREAT HEIGHT)

KEY:

🏠 THE VICARAGE

[7AM] CHURCH, AND THE TIME
OF THE SERVICE THEREIN

🪑 MRS JENKINS, WHO LIKES
TO BE PICKED UP IN PLENTY
OF TIME FOR THE SERVICE
AND TO BE PICKED UP AFTER
SHE HAS HAD COFFEE

🔆 SUNRISE (OBSERVED BRIEFLY)

🌑 ROSES IN VICARAGE GARDEN
(TENDED BRIEFLY)

🛶 NOAH'S ARK (CARDBOARD
REPLICA FOR ALL-AGE SLOT)

🚗🚓 "I AM SORRY OFFICER,
I WAS LATE AND THE RUBRICS
DEMAND THAT I
FINISH THE WINE"

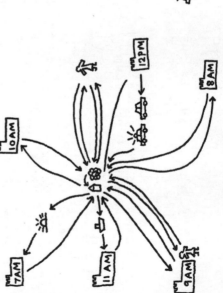

SABBATICALS

EVERY TEN YEARS OR SO VICARS WHO HAVE BEEN GOOD CAN GO ON A SABBATICAL. THIS CAN INVOLVE:

LEARNING A NEW SKILL

A TIME OF STUDY

...FLIGHT TO IBIZA IS NOW BOARDING...

A VISIT TO A DIOCESE OVERSEAS

NIGHTCLUB

SEEKING TO UNDERSTAND MODERN CULTURE

A TIME OF SPIRITUAL REFRESHMENT INVOLVING EXPOSURE TO AN UNFAMILIAR FORM OF SPIRITUALITY

TATTOOS PIERCINGS

IDENTIFYING WITH "THE YOUTH"

SAFETY IN CHURCH

THESE ARE SOME OF THE DANGERS THAT YOU MUST BE AWARE OF:

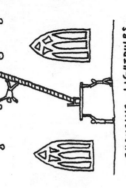

CHANGING LIGHTBULBS

DEATH BY OVEREXCITEMENT

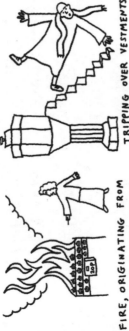

TRIPPING OVER VESTMENTS ON PULPIT STEPS

BEING RUN DOWN BY A PROCESSION

FIRE, ORIGINATING FROM THE CANDLE STAND

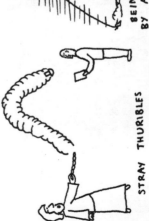

STRAY THURIBLES

SAYING THE GRACE

THE GRACE, WORDS TAKEN FROM 2 CORINTHIANS CHAPTER 13 VERSE 14, IS QUITE OFTEN SAID IN CHURCH. THERE ARE TWO SCHOOLS OF THOUGHT WHEN IT COMES TO SAYING THE GRACE:

MAY THE GRACE OF OUR LORD JESUS CHRIST...

THE GRACE IS QUITE CLEARLY A PRAYER, SO IT SHOULD BE SAID WITH EYES CLOSED WHILST ADOPTING A DEEPLY PRAYERFUL ATTITUDE

THE GRACE IS QUITE CLEARLY SUPPOSED TO BE SAID TO OTHER PEOPLE, SO IT SHOULD BE SAID WHILST LOOKING AROUND THE ROOM AND GRINNING INANELY

SERMONS
EXPLAINED IN GRAPHICAL FORM

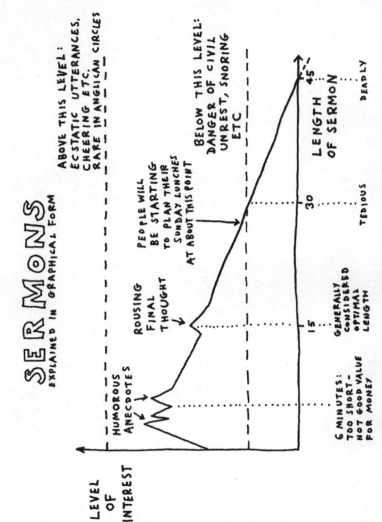

LEVEL OF INTEREST

ABOVE THIS LEVEL: ECSTATIC UTTERANCES, CHEERING ETC. RARE IN ANGLICAN CIRCLES

HUMOROUS ANECDOTES

ROUSING FINAL THOUGHT

PEOPLE WILL BE STARTING TO PLAN THEIR SUNDAY LUNCHES AT ABOUT THIS POINT

BELOW THIS LEVEL: DANGER OF CIVIL UNREST, SNORING ETC

6 MINUTES: TOO SHORT - NOT GOOD VALUE FOR MONEY

GENERALLY CONSIDERED OPTIMAL LENGTH

TEDIOUS

DEADLY

15   30   45

LENGTH OF SERMON

SERVICE BOOKS

1662 PRAYER BOOK
QUITE OLD
SO HANDLE
WITH CARE

ASB
ALTERNATIVE
SERVICE BOOK
IT IS ILLEGAL TO
USE THIS SO DO
NOT DO IT

COMMON WORSHIP
SO CALLED
BECAUSE IT IS
USED IN A
LOT OF PLACES

UNAUTHORIZED
VERSIONS
WE CANNOT SHOW
THESE FOR
LEGAL
REASONS

THERE IS A MAN
WHO HAS 7 MILLION
COPIES OF THE ASB
STORED IN THIS
WAREHOUSE.

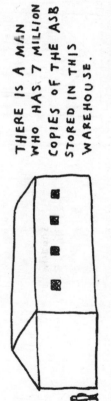

IF IT EVER COMES BACK HE WILL MAKE A FORTUNE

SIDESPERSONS

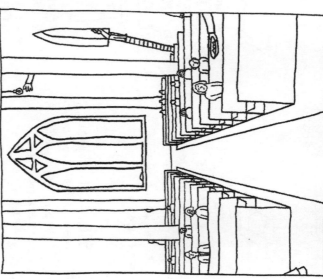

THESE ARE A SPECIAL
CLASS OF PEOPLE
WHO LURK UNSEEN
DURING THE SERVICE
BUT THEN SPRING-
FORTH AT MOMENTS
OF LITURGICAL OR
PRACTICAL NEED

SIDESPERSONS OFTEN
GO UNDETECTED BY
THE UNTRAINED EYE

HOW MANY CAN
YOU SPOT IN
THIS PICTURE?

SMALL CHILDREN

CHILDREN OF ALL AGES ARE WELCOME AT CHURCH.
EACH HAS THEIR OWN UNIQUE CONTRIBUTION TO
BRING TO THE LIFE OF THE WORSHIPPING COMMUNITY

W ALMIGHTY A GOD A TO A WHOM A ALL A HEARTS A

A ARE A OPEN A ALL A DESIRES A KNOWN A AND A

A FROM A WHOM A NO A SECRETS A ARE A HIDDEN A

A CLEANSE A THE A THOUGHTS A OF A OUR A HEARTS H...

STEEPLES AND TOWERS: THE PROS AND CONS

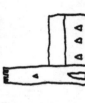

STEEPLE

MORE POINTY

YOU CAN'T STAND ON TOP

RAIN RUNS OFF EASILY

YOU GET ONE OF THESE ON A MAP ✝

TO CLEAN THE TOP YOU NEED TO
BE GOOD AT CLIMBING

THE VIEW FROM THE WINDOW HALF
WAY UP IS DISAPPOINTING

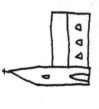

TOWER

NOT SO POINTY

YOU CAN STAND ON TOP

THERE IS A DANGER OF PUDDLES
ON TOP

YOU GET ONE OF THESE ON A MAP ✝

TO CLEAN THE TOP YOU CAN
USE THE STAIRS

THE TURRETS PROVIDE OPPORTUNITIES
FOR MISCHIEF

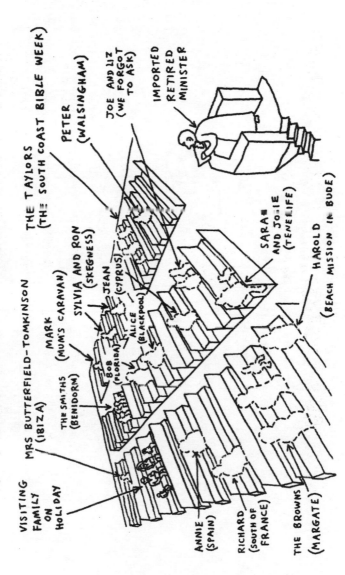

THE SUMMER HOLIDAYS

THE FAITHFUL REMNANT REMEMBER THE DEARLY DEPARTED

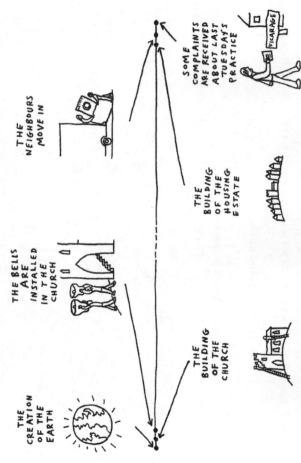

THE PARISH SYSTEM

THE ENTIRE COUNTRY IS DIVIDED INTO PARISHES.
EACH ONE HAS ITS OWN CHURCH. EVERYBODY GOES
TO THEIR LOCAL PARISH CHURCH*

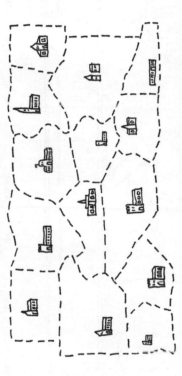

*UNLESS IT IS TOO HIGH, TOO LOW, TOO LIBERAL, TOO EVANGELICAL,
TOO CATHOLIC, TOO MIDDLE OF THE ROAD, TOO UNBIBLICAL, HAS TOO
MANY BELLS AND SMELLS, HAS TOO MANY SMELLS, HAS SERMONS THAT
ARE TOO LONG, HAS TOO MANY CHILDREN, HAS NOT ENOUGH CHILDREN,
HAS NO SUNDAY SCHOOL, HAS MUSIC THAT IS TOO OLD FASHIONED,
HAS MUSIC THAT IS TOO HAPPY CLAPPY, HAS A VICAR WHO IS A
WOMAN, HAS A VICAR WHO IS A MAN, HAS A VICAR WHO IS A BIT ODD,
HAS SERVICES THAT START TOO EARLY IN THE MORNING, HAS REALLY
BAD COFFEE AFTER THE SERVICES, HAS PARTICULARLY UNCOMFORTABLE
PEWS, HAS SERVICES THAT CLASH WITH SUNDAY LUNCH PREPARATION
TIME, HAS SERVICES THAT DON'T USE THE BOOK OF COMMON PRAYER,
HAS SERVICES THAT DO USE THE BOOK OF COMMON PRAYER OR ISN'T
THE CHURCH ASSOCIATED WITH THE PRIMARY SCHOOL THEY HAD IN MIND

THE PEACE

THIS IS A TIME DURING THE SERVICE WHICH IS SET ASIDE FOR PEOPLE TO BE NICE TO ONE ANOTHER. DIFFERENT PEOPLE SHARE THE PEACE IN DIFFERENT WAYS:

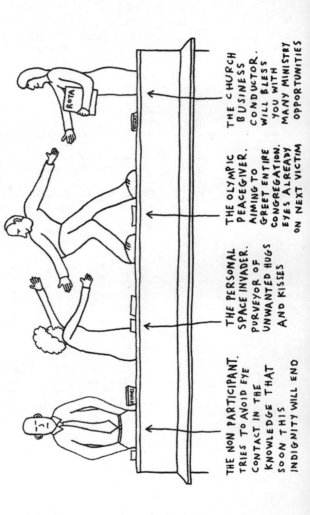

THE NON PARTICIPANT. TRIES TO AVOID EYE CONTACT IN THE KNOWLEDGE THAT SOON THIS INDIGNITY WILL END

THE PERSONAL SPACE INVADER. PURVEYOR OF UNWANTED HUGS AND KISSES

THE OLYMPIC PEACEGIVER. AIMING TO GREET ENTIRE CONGREGATION. EYES ALREADY ON NEXT VICTIM

THE CHURCH BUSINESS CONDUCTOR. WILL BLESS YOU WITH MANY MINISTRY OPPORTUNITIES

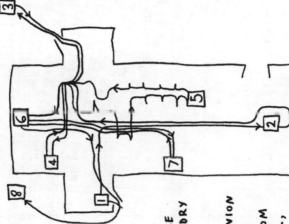

THE SERVICE
WHERE THE VICAR GOES

1 IN THE VESTRY CHOOSING OUTFITS

2 PROCESSING AROUND A BIT

3 GOING TO THE VICARAGE TO RETRIEVE LOST SERMON

4 IN THE PULPIT

5 SHARING THE PEACE WITH ALL AND SUNDRY

6 AT THE ALTAR

7 OFFERING COMMUNION TO THE INFIRM

8 HEADING AWAY FROM THE CHURCH HALL, WHERE COFFEE IS BEING SERVED

TRACTS

MOST CHURCHES COMMUNICATE TO VISITORS VIA A DISPLAY OF
TRACTS AND LEAFLETS AT THE BACK ON A TABLE. THESE ARE
SOME OF THE MESSAGES THEY ARE INTENDING TO CONVEY

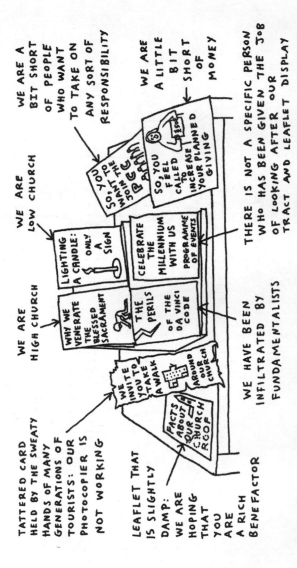

TATTERED CARD
HELD BY THE SWEATY
HANDS OF MANY
GENERATIONS OF
TOURISTS: OUR
PHOTOCOPIER IS
NOT WORKING

WE ARE
HIGH CHURCH

WE ARE
LOW CHURCH

WE ARE A
BIT SHORT
OF PEOPLE
WHO WANT
TO TAKE ON
ANY SORT OF
RESPONSIBILITY

WE ARE
A LITTLE
BIT
SHORT
OF
MONEY

SO, YOU
WANT THE
JOIN THE
PCC

SO, YOU
FEEL
CALLED TO
INCREASE
YOUR PLANNED
GIVING

LIGHTING
A CANDLE:
ONLY
A
SIGN

CELEBRATE
THE
MILLENNIUM
WITH US
PROGRAMME
OF EVENTS

WHY WE
VENERATE
THE
BLESSED
SACRAMENT

THE
PERILS
OF THE
DA VINCI
CODE

THERE IS NOT A SPECIFIC PERSON
WHO HAS BEEN GIVEN THE JOB
OF LOOKING AFTER OUR
TRACT AND LEAFLET DISPLAY

WE INVITE
YOU TO
TAKE
A WALK

FACTS
ABOUT
OUR
CHURCH
ROOF

AROUND
OUR
CHURCH

WE HAVE BEEN
INFILTRATED BY
FUNDAMENTALISTS

LEAFLET THAT
IS SLIGHTLY
DAMP:
WE ARE
HOPING
THAT
YOU
ARE
A RICH
BENEFACTOR

THE VESTRY

THIS IS WHAT YOU WILL FIND:

CRIB SCENE.
GATHERING DUST ALL YEAR FOR AN AUTHENTIC RUSTIC LOOK

CLERGY CHANGING.— OBVIOUSLY WE HAVE HAD TO DRAW A VEIL OVER THIS ACTIVITY

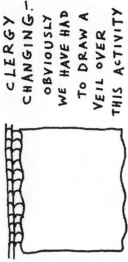

ASSORTED PEDESTALS (PROPERTY OF THE FLOWER LADIES)

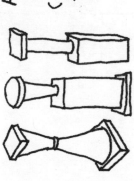

ADDITIONAL STORAGE FOR THE BROWNIES

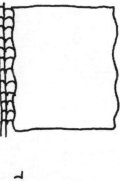

THE VICAR'S LETTER

VICARS GENERALLY WRITE ONE OF THESE EVERY MONTH
IN THE PARISH MAGAZINE. WE CAN LEARN QUITE A
LOT FROM THE SUBJECT MATTER:

THE VICAR HAS
BEEN ON TOO
MANY COURSES

THE VICAR HAS
BEEN FOR TOO
MANY WALKS

THE VICAR IS SLACKING
OFF A BIT OR THE
CURATE IS A DESPOT

THE VICAR HAS
BOUGHT A NEW
CLIPART COLLECTION

PEOPLE HAVE NOT
BEEN GETTING
ALONG TOGETHER

THE CONGREGATION
WERE ASLEEP

TO BE A VICAR

IT IS IMPORTANT TO LIKE THE FOLLOWING DRINKS

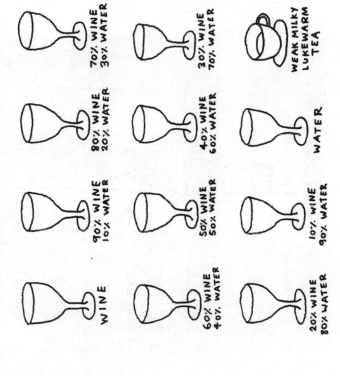

WINE

90% WINE
10% WATER

80% WINE
20% WATER

70% WINE
30% WATER

60% WINE
40% WATER

50% WINE
50% WATER

40% WINE
60% WATER

30% WINE
70% WATER

20% WINE
80% WATER

10% WINE
90% WATER

WATER

WEAK MILKY
LUKEWARM
TEA

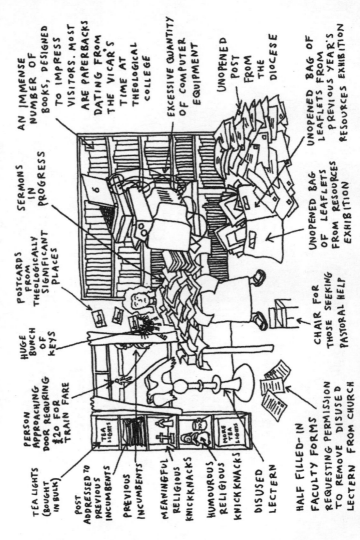

THE VICAR'S STUDY

AN IMMENSE NUMBER OF BOOKS, DESIGNED TO IMPRESS VISITORS. MOST ARE PAPERBACKS DATING FROM THE VICAR'S TIME AT THEOLOGICAL COLLEGE

SERMONS IN PROGRESS

EXCESSIVE QUANTITY OF COMPUTER EQUIPMENT

UNOPENED POST FROM THE DIOCESE

UNOPENED BAG OF LEAFLETS FROM PREVIOUS YEAR'S RESOURCES EXHIBITION

POSTCARDS FROM THEOLOGICALLY SIGNIFICANT PLACES

UNOPENED BAG OF LEAFLETS FROM RESOURCES EXHIBITION

PERSON APPROACHING DOOR REQUIRING $20 FOR TRAIN FARE

HUGE BUNCH OF KEYS

CHAIR FOR THOSE SEEKING PASTORAL HELP

TEA LIGHTS (BOUGHT IN BULK)

POST ADDRESSED TO PREVIOUS INCUMBENTS

PREVIOUS INCUMBENTS

MEANINGFUL RELIGIOUS KNICKKNACKS

HUMOUROUS RELIGIOUS KNICK KNACKS

DISUSED LECTERN

HALF FILLED-IN FACULTY FORMS REQUESTING PERMISSION TO REMOVE DISUSED LECTERN FROM CHURCH

THE VIEW FROM THE PULPIT

POTENTIAL HOME GROUP LEADER

SHOULD CONSIDER ORDAINED MINISTRY

WE NEED SOMEONE TO CO-ORDINATE THE FLOWER ROTA

COULD MAKE A GREAT CHURCH TREASURER

COULD HEAL THE RIFT IN THE ANGLICAN COMMUNION, PERHAPS

WHAT THE CLERGY DO ALL WEEK

WHAT
THE
CLERGY
DO

WHAT
THE
PARISHIONERS
THINK
THE
CLERGY
DO

WHAT THE
CLERGY
THINK THE
PARISHIONERS
THINK THE
CLERGY DO

WHAT THE
PARISHIONERS
THINK THE
CLERGY THINK
THE PARISHIONERS
THINK THE
CLERGY DO

GO TO CHURCH, PRAY ETC

PREPARE SERMONS

GO TO MEETINGS

VISIT THE SICK

HELP PEOPLE BE BORN,
GET MARRIED AND DIE

SURF THE INTERNET

PLAY GOLF

KEEP UP TO DATE WITH
POPULAR CULTURE (TV, MUSIC ETC)

NOTHING

TO BE HONEST IT IS NOT
SOMETHING I HAVE SPENT
MUCH TIME THINKING ABOUT

WHAT YOUR PEW SAYS ABOUT YOU

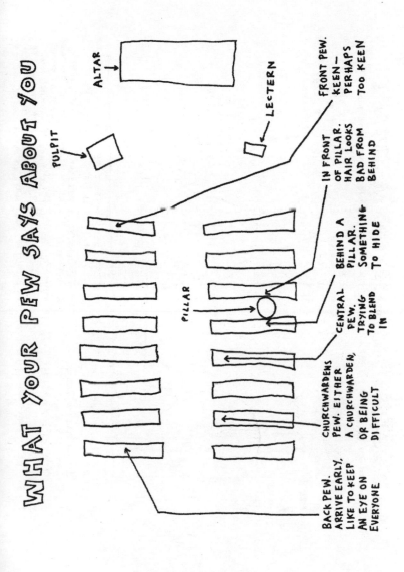

PULPIT

ALTAR

LECTERN

FRONT PEW. KEEN— PERHAPS TOO KEEN

IN FRONT OF PILLAR. HAIR LOOKS BAD FROM BEHIND

BEHIND A PILLAR. SOMETHING TO HIDE

PILLAR

CENTRAL PEW. TRYING TO BLEND IN

CHURCHWARDENS PEW. EITHER A CHURCHWARDEN, OR BEING DIFFICULT

BACK PEW. ARRIVE EARLY. LIKE TO KEEP AN EYE ON EVERYONE

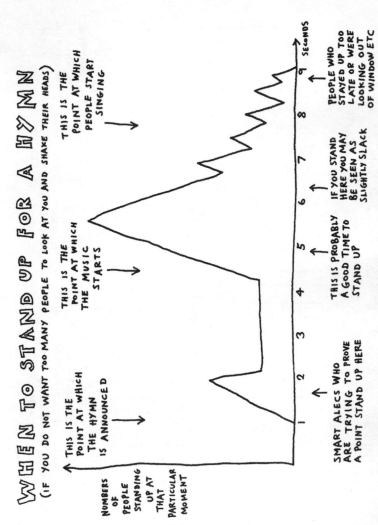

WHEN TO STAND UP FOR A HYMN
(IF YOU DO NOT WANT TOO MANY PEOPLE TO LOOK AT YOU AND SHAKE THEIR HEADS)

THIS IS THE POINT AT WHICH THE HYMN IS ANNOUNCED

THIS IS THE POINT AT WHICH THE MUSIC STARTS

THIS IS THE POINT AT WHICH PEOPLE START SINGING

NUMBERS OF PEOPLE STANDING UP AT THAT PARTICULAR MOMENT

SECONDS

SMART ALECS WHO ARE TRYING TO PROVE A POINT STAND UP HERE

THIS IS PROBABLY A GOOD TIME TO STAND UP

IF YOU STAND HERE YOU MAY BE SEEN AS SLIGHTLY SLACK

PEOPLE WHO STAYED UP TOO LATE OR WERE LOOKING OUT OF WINDOW ETC

NOTE: IF THE INTRODUCTION IS LONG AND RAMBLING YOU WILL HAVE TO MAKE AN ADJUSTMENT

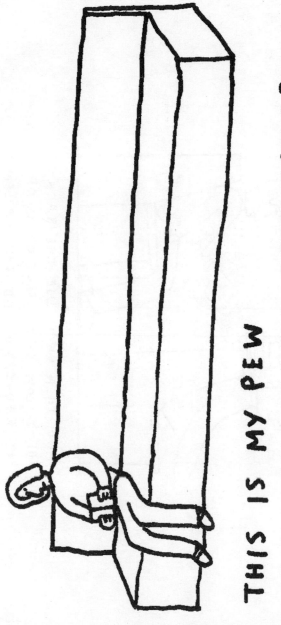

THIS IS MY PEW
THIS HAS ALWAYS BEEN MY PEW

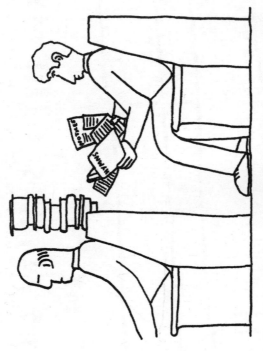

"AND THEN WE'LL USE THE BACK OF THE YELLOW SHEET, SECTION 2 OF THE RED CARD AND THE SUPPLEMENT AT THE BACK OF THE BLUE BOOK..."

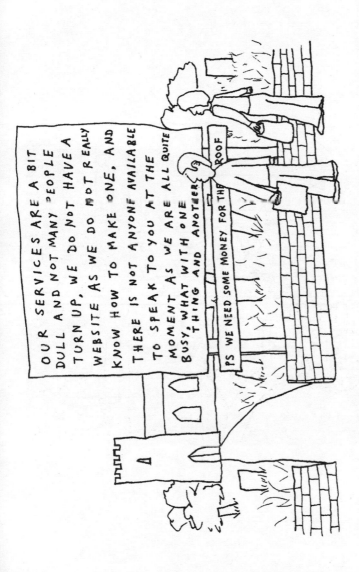

WE DO NOT NEED TO GET SOMEONE IN TO HELP US WITH MARKETING
OUR CHURCH AS WE ARE PERFECTLY ABLE TO DO IT OURSELVES

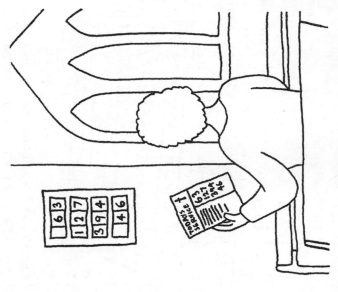

SHE COULD HARDLY BELIEVE SHE HAD
WON ON HER FIRST VISIT TO CHURCH

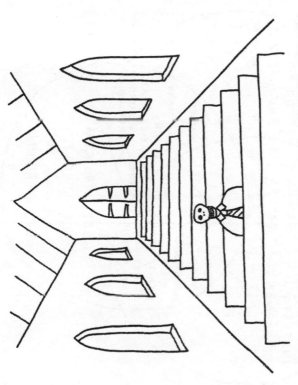

HE HAD BEEN THERE FOR FOUR YEARS,
BUT THE OTHER CHURCHGOERS ASSUMED
HE ARRIVED EARLY AND LEFT LATE

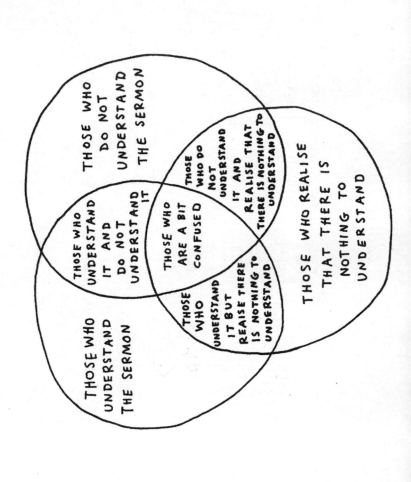

IT IS THE DUTY OF THE CHURCHWARDENS TO CO-ORDINATE RESPONSES TO THE FOLLOWING WATER LEVELS

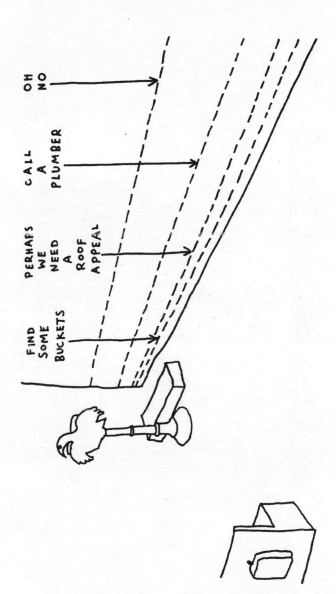

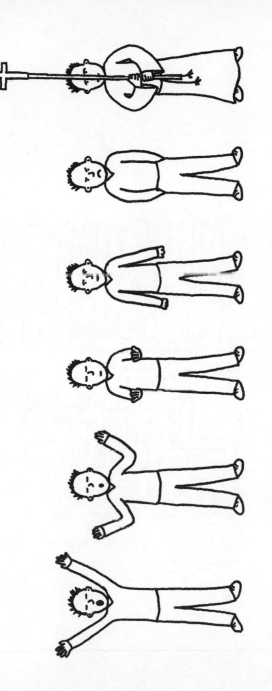

THE EVOLUTION OF A WORSHIPPER

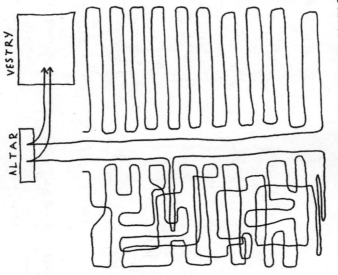

THE JOURNEY OF THE COLLECTION PLATES
IN A CHURCH WHERE ALL OF THE STUPID
PEOPLE SIT ON THE LEFT

HOW TO MAKE IT KNOWN THAT YOU ARE HOLIER THAN THOSE AROUND YOU IN CHURCH, IF INDEED YOU ARE HOLIER THAN THOSE AROUND YOU

WALK UP TO COMMUNION WITH YOUR HANDS TOGETHER, WHILST THOSE AROUND YOU KEEP THEM BY THEIR SIDES

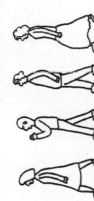

BOW AND PROSTRATE YOURSELF AT PARTICULAR POINTS IN THE LITURGY, WHILST THOSE AROUND YOU SAY THE RESPONSES IN A PRAYERFUL MANNER

DO OBSCURE AND EMBARRASSING ACTIONS, WHILST THOSE AROUND YOU SING THE SONG IN A SENSIBLE FASHION

RAISE YOUR HAND DURING THE SINGING OF A SOLEMN HYMN, WHILST THOSE AROUND YOU RETAIN A DIGNIFIED GRASP UPON THEIR HYMN BOOKS

86

I HAVE CROSSED MYSELF
WITH THE ANGLO-CATHOLICS

I HAVE QUESTIONED
WITH THE LIBERALS

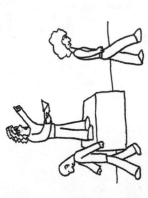

I HAVE EVANGELISED
WITH THE EVANGELICALS

I HAVE WORSHIPPED
WITH THE CHARISMATICS

I NOW FIND MYSELF
SLIGHTLY CONFUSED,
BUT I HAVE MET SOME
LOVELY PEOPLE ALONG
THE WAY

IF ANYONE CAN THINK
OF WAYS THAT I CAN
POLITELY EXCUSE MYSELF
FROM SOME OF THE ROTAS
I NOW FIND MYSELF
ON I WOULD VERY MUCH
APPRECIATE HEARING FROM
THEM

A LOT OF PEOPLE ARE NOW GOING BACK TO CHURCH ONCE AGAIN

THIS IS USUALLY BECAUSE THEY HAVE FORGOTTEN SOMETHING LIKE THEIR KEYS OR JACKET OR GLASSES

WORLD MAP SHOWING THE ESTIMATED LOCATIONS OF CARTOONISTS WHO HAVE DRAWN PICTURES MAKING A MOCKERY OF CLERGY VESTMENTS AND HAVE BEEN FORCED INTO HIDING AS A RESULT

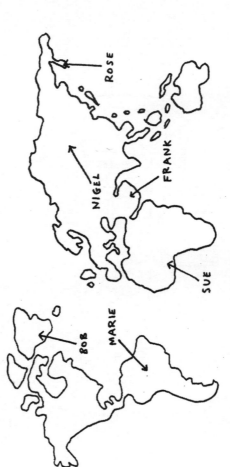

ROSE
NIGEL
FRANK
SUE
BOB
MARIE

UNACCOUNTED FOR AT THE PRESENT TIME:

HANK   ARCHIE   RUTH
SAM   HELEN   JOE